D1594343

TREMBLE

Tremble

C.D. WRIGHT

THE ECCO PRESS

THE ECCO PRESS
100 WEST BROAD STREET
HOPEWELL, NEW JERSEY 08525

PUBLISHED SIMULTANEOUSLY IN
CANADA BY PENGUIN BOOKS CANADA LTD., ONTARIO
PRINTED IN THE UNITED STATES OF AMERICA

GRATEFUL ACKNOWLEDGMENT
IS DUE TO THE FOLLOWING PUBLICATIONS
IN WHICH SOME OF THESE POEMS OR
VERSIONS THEREOF ORIGINALLY APPEARED:

*American Letters and Commentary, The American
Poetry Review, The Apostle's Bar, Arshile, Brown Alumnae
Monthly, Chelsea, Colorado Review, Epoch, Field, Five Fingers Review,
Organica, Phoebe, The Prose Poem, rooms, Southern
Review, Torque, Volt, The World.*

LIBRARY OF CONGRESS
CATALOGING-IN-PUBLICATION DATA

WRIGHT, C.D., 1949-
TREMBLE / C.D. WRIGHT. — 1ST ECCO ED.
P. CM.
ISBN 0-88001-458-X (CLOTH)
ISBN 0-88001-512-8 (PAPERBACK)
I. TITLE.
PS3573.R497T74 1996
811'.54—DC20   95-44779

DESIGNED BY MARK ARGETSINGER

THE TEXT OF THIS BOOK IS SET IN MONOTYPE BELL

9 8 7 6 5 4 3 2 1
FIRST EDITION

For Forrest: At Ten

Could not life continue on earth without wind
or must everything tremble, always, always?

—MICHAUX

CONTENTS

TREMBLE

Floating Trees

a bed is left open to a mirror
a mirror gazes long and hard at a bed

light fingers the house with its own acoustics

one of them writes this down
one has paper

bed of swollen creeks and theories and coils
bed of eyes and leaky pens

much of the night the air touches arms
arms extend themselves to air

their torsos turning toward a roll
of sound: thunder

night of coon scat and vandalized headstones
night of deep kisses and catamenia

his face by this light: saurian
hers: ash like the tissue of a hornet's nest

one scans the aisle of firs
the faint blue line of them
one looks out: sans serif

"Didn't I hear you tell them you were born
on a train"

what begins with a sough and ends with a groan
groan in which the tongue's true color is revealed

the comb's sough and the denim's undeniable rub
the chair's stripped back and muddied rung

color of stone soup and garden gloves
color of meal and treacle and sphagnum

hangers clinging to their coat
a soft white bulb to its string

the footprints inside us
iterate the footprints outside

the scratched words return to their sleeves

the dresses of monday through friday
swallow the long hips of weekends

a face is studied like a key
for the mystery of what it once opened

"I didn't mean to wake you
angel brains"

ink of eyes and veins and phonemes
the ink completes the feeling

a mirror silently facing a door
door with no lock no lock

the room he brings into you
the room befalls you

like the fir trees he trues her
she nears him like the firs

if one vanishes one stays
if one stays the other will or will not vanish

otherwise my beautiful green fly
otherwise not a leaf stirs

Approximately Forever

She was changing on the inside
it was true what had been written

The new syntax of love
both sucked and burned

The secret clung around them
She took in the smell

Walking down a road to nowhere
every sound was relevant

The sun fell behind them now
he seemed strangely moved

She would take her clothes off
for the camera

she said in plain english
but she wasn't holding that snake

So Far Off and Yet Here

Because I know this is going to be painful
I can feel the pain before it acquires a shape

Now nearer to me

How at night it is just audible
like mice in the insulation

So windows snow and pears soften
an old house settles into its infested studs

Always there is more inside
than outside in the open

Where I came to be identified with
your scars and green limbs

Now nearer to me

What in the meantime happened to my eyes
they shone   at least   they seemed capable   of shine

But a poem on a page by itself
does not penetrate the retina of fear

Now nearer to me

7

So the mind dispels us
radiators gasp and washers wear out

Your left middle finger sinks inside me
the nail of love just holds

Like Peaches

change   speak   sway
keep lingering smell
protected by a succulent seal   a burr
yield one's earthly wand   one's earthly sac   into this vessel
trace   blaze   clear
the foliage at the wrought gate
the serrated tongue   rescinded   along with the dream
of urinating in three streams
sunscalded

Forever Lynne   riddles the water tower   of a dying town
ripen   cling   drop
what would it be like to fell   this mess of twigs   to graft
the shaking body   to lyric   the seasoned body   to stem
to shake   the lyric body   to season
the stemmed   to trail   the fallen . . .
slather   shudder   lower
drupe

things that are not written in this book
don't go boring your nose in the fork of a tree not even present
arise   refreshed   wormed
pulpy   opaque   ecstatic

               lingering innocence
of perfect nexus   shave the epicarp   collect the juices
              we orchard

With Grass as Their Witness

Not more lonely than the road
    the women that loved him
Not more beautiful than the road
    the men that loved him
He came in behind the rain
    seated himself under your trees
Clutching his genitals in one hand
    he emptied his green mind
    How beautiful were those men
whose tongues went over the ridge
    of his balls How lonely
the water left standing in the road

Because Fulfillment Awaits

An arm reaching back through a hole in a ceiling
for a box of poison   "Now"   the dark talks
"I hate being a man"   An arm offering a box of poison
in the direction   of a hole in a ceiling
A handkerchief offered   "Wait"
comes the warning from below   "Cover yourself"

Even in touching   retouching
steeped in words   in the proliferation and cancellation
of words   one tends to forget   one forgets
the face   the human face   One wants
to create a bright   new past   one creates it

Autographs

This is blood: close with your lover and bite down
Bear in mind: this is a duet
I'll drive: shift your excellent body under mine
Ideal environment: lush, well-lubricated
Neighborhood of origin: sells cigarettes, schnapps, lotto tickets
Weather: late ozark spring
Soft entry: it can be done
Strangest device: cock rings
Preferred intervention: human hand
Source of common terror: retina
Wish: to never know unhappiness again
State flower: bearded iris

Site of their desire: against a long high wall under vapor light
Most likely to succeed: the perpetual starting over
Inside his mouth: night after night after night
Directive: by any means necessary
Song: "Anarchy in the UK"
Sign: hibiscus falls off the ledge
Nightmare: actual horse seated on your ribs
Sonic relations: silent, breathy, ululant

Recurrent fantasy: trickling between his legs
Cutest ass: bend, cleave
Religion: against my fire
Kismet: I feel very fortunate
Abstraction: leaves out too much
Biggest flirt: some people have roman noses,
    some have roman hands
Secondary concern: depilation

Eau de toilette: white shoulders
Rambone: I need it I need it now
Back of her throat: slit light
Wish: compassion
Depth: valley's proper
Other sites: corridor, phone booth, shower, elevator,
    locker, filling station, boat dock, drive-in, cafeteria line
Most unlikely position: autumn dog
Regrets: all the dumb things I've done

Saving grace: clear out of own accord
Goal: revanchism
Plans for the future: to be a great success socially and
    in some artistic calling
Third wish: that his fingers remain agile
Future: went kind of nuts when still a relatively young man

Last date: when he stopped touching her, Jan 4
Best dancer: hands down
Mantra: no one has been hurt, no one has been killed

PS: have a wonderful summer and a wonderful life

And It Came to Pass

This june 3rd
would be different

Time to draw lines

I've grown into the family pores
and the bronchitis

Even up east
I get by saying goddamnit

Who was that masked man
I left for dead
in the shadow of mt. shadow

Who crumbles there

Not touching anything
but satin and dandelions

Not laid his eye
on the likes of you

Because the unconnected life
is not worth living

Thorntrees overtake the spot

Hands appear to push back pain

Because no poet's death

Can be the sole author
of another poet's life

What will my new instrument be

Just this water glass
this untunable spoon

Something else is out there
goddamnit

And I want to hear it

Girl Friend

When I first saw her a few summers ago I felt.
                    Her photogenic spit.
I was climbing a coruscating staircase.
In my flammable skin. To be so full of.
Everything. At her age. It is very difficult.
A singer manqué. Among a small host of poets.
                    Noisier
than the men. Quaffing schnapps. No lens
could describe her.
                    Shoulders. Hands.
Such longings: Errant. Verdant.
To have a good time. And dream. In one's own
country. The lack. Of. Everything.
The confusion. It is very difficult. One needs.
One's own set of golden books. What if.
A ladder were. Miraculous. Extended. Across
a nursery for new stars.
                    And then.

for nina

18

Sonic Relations

In the space of an ear
she told him the uncut version
in all but inaudible detail
without motors without phones
he gathered round her
like books like chairs
her warmth her terrible warmth
flooded the tone

That summer she began again
my sunflowers stood as tall
as girls on ladders
she mentioned ralph and fire
twice she mentioned ralph
and the fire
across an azimuth of space
her warmth her terrible warmth
flooded the tone

She paused he was sweating
as though he had transported her
on his shoulders the whole summer
all over the county

she looked at him like some hair
she kept wrapped in cloth
doors slammed a book fell
he gathered round her

Her warmth her terrible warmth
flooded the tone
without motors without phones
he saw ralph then and the fire
in all but inaudible detail
he looked at her
like some combs he kept
wrapped in cloth

"We love it here" she said
"The girls are glad
the sunflowers and ladders
even the broom the eggs are glad
the air is so sweet
the water is sweet"
she looked at him
across an azimuth of space
he gathered round her
her warmth her terrible warmth

Various Positions

It was getting on toward supper time

It was his night off

A shoe dropped

It had nothing whatsoever to do with you

It was an efficiency apartment

The breast seeks its own level

The table got down on its knees

With an amaryllis at their sill

They assume late spring donkey

It was stifling

It is the hair that makes it so mysterious

A book of matches goes off in her shirt

He wants nothing more than to sleep

Inside her holster

The chair fell to pieces

On the eve of the eighth day

Her milk came in

The Shepherd of Resumed Desire

one steps forward   under a sifter of light
holding a globe   in ungloved hands   we share
the experience   of dying   in snow   pages turn
on illuminated fragments   we become   aware
of the extremes: joy   and   revenge   the fierce
confusion therein   one form senses another
when there is pressure   from all sides   and wasn't the light
seminal   tilting toward us   nay,   labial
we knew from the start   the center was within us   this blizzard
this conversation   could go on   for years: should you

go   should you stay   no shoulds about it   no matter why
the hole was made   the task is not yours   to fill it
why standest thou   so near   to the brink   how old were you
when you first lay down   before the god of love   what was
the objective: a staff   against the wolf   of reality
nay,   to get warm   only to get warm   would you be
let down again   if I said   it were not the one true god
but only a candle   of the same   where were we in the middle of a phrase: we froze we fell we went to a gilded hell
I only have escaped to tell you   though I have come to be lost
I do not ask you to lose your own self   in my triangle   only

to keep watch   yea,   to keep watch   over the shaping
    of the sky   snow orbiting   all   abide abide

Oneness

As surely as it is about air
    about light and about earth

Water will seep between fingers
    gathered in a gentle fist

For what good a wooden fence
    against breath fuming with fire

What good to point out the flower path
    if the sugar bag is empty

What good blowing the clarinet
    if blowing only makes one ugly

For as surely as wind unlocks
    car doors and cabinets

Young men wander off with their testes
    to part the perineum's grasses

And when they come to the little stream
    each tenses against the other

And against anything unforeseen
    and under each pair of skin

She discovers his unassailable otherness
    and under each pair of skin

He discovers her moisture, dark, fecundity
    for as surely as it is about air

About light and about earth
    gathered in a gentle fist

Water will seep between fingers
    for the unknown must remain unknown

I know that and you know that
    flesh of my flesh, bone of my bone

Gift of the Book

lights go off
all over
rhode island
everyone falls
into bed
I stay awake
reading
re-reading
the long-awaited
prose
of your
body
stunned
by the hunger

Girl Friend Poem #2

Awake ye and come to our house
Come running   fly if you can

The doors throw themselves open
The name for this part is hearth

Today is the best day since yesterday
We share   a sense of rivers

Amazed at what we saw
We thought we were dreaming

The eyes the eyes
The golden domes they've beheld

The annihilating smile
The year you married the falcon

Here an hour follows an hour
One glass of wine deserves more

So it is not paradise
Everybody enters the green

At nightfall   modestly clad
Calling their children

Everybody has somebody
For whom to cry

for frances

A Series of Actions

Like someone who has given

The gift of blood

The skin of the face is shining

Arms fold around each other

A string leads the way

Cold is the floor that receives
    the feet

The movements by which one
    accedes to the door

The handle inscribed in the hand

The door opening on the scene
    of shoelaces eyelashes

The left hand keeps it focused

The door opening on the living
    almost unbearable

Light inside the space

The door opening as the palm
of an eye

Song of the Gourd

In gardening I continued to sit on my side of the car: to
drive whenever possible at the usual level of distraction:
in gardening I shat nails glass contaminated dirt and
threw up on the new shoots: in gardening I learned to
praise things I had dreaded: I pushed the hair out of my
face: I felt less responsible for one man's death one
woman's long-term isolation: my bones softened: in
gardening I lost nickels and ring settings I uncovered
buttons and marbles: I lay half the worm aside and
sought the rest: I sought myself in the bucket and wondered why I came into being in the first place: in gardening I turned away from the television and went
around smelling of offal the inedible parts of the
chicken: in gardening I said excelsior: in gardening I re-
quired no company I had to forgive my own failure to
perceive how things were: I went out barelegged at
dusk and dug and dug and dug: I hit rock my ovaries
softened: in gardening I was protean as in no other
realm before or since: I longed to torch my old belong-
ings and belch a little flame of satisfaction: in gardening
I longed to stroll farther into soundlessness: I could al-
most forget what happened many swift years ago in

32

arkansas: I felt like a god from down under: chthonian: in gardening I thought this is it body and soul I am home at last: excelsior: praise the grass: in gardening I fled the fold that supported the war: only in gardening could I stop shrieking: stop: stop the slaughter: only in gardening could I press my ear to the ground to hear my soul let out an unyielding noise: my lines softened: I turned the water onto the joy-filled boychild: only in gardening did I feel fit to partake to go on trembling in the last light: I confess the abject urge to weed your beds while the bittersweet overwhelmed my daylilies: I summoned the courage to grin: I climbed the hill with my bucket and slept like a dipper in the cool of your body: besotted with growth; shot through by green

Lake Echo, Dear

Is the woman in the pool of light
really reading or just staring
at what is written

Is the man walking in the soft rain
naked or is it the rain
that makes his shirt transparent

The boy in the iron cot
is he asleep or still
fingering the springs underneath

Did you honestly believe
three lives could be complete

The bottle of green liquid
on the sill is it real

The bottle on the peeling sill
is it filled with green

Or is the liquid an illusion
of fullness

How summer's children turn

into fish and rain softens men

how the elements of summer
nights bid us get down with each other
on the unplaned floor

And this feels painfully beautiful
whether or not
it will change the world one drop

On the Beach

"I cannot help you"   was the message
inside the green bottle   her footprints
dissolving in dry sand   to the spaces
between words   she assigned various meanings
the father flew   toward the daughter
his terrestrial body borne lightly by its cushion
clutching a poke of tomatoes on his knee
alone   with the beating of his own heart
        he didn't really mind living

        in the unseasonal heat
of her kitchen she held the pitcher of tea
against her cheek   wanting a breeze
the miniature wheel by the bed   ceased
to spin   "Courage and sex"   he said
setting his poke down   at last   "Caroline,
is all love is"   finally   with a faint sound
as a loneliness sewn by hand   the wing
sheared away   finally the loneliness   sheared
        away   as a wing sewn by hand

What Keeps

We live on a hillside
close to water
We eat in darkness
We sleep in the coldest
part of the house
We love in silence
We keep our poetry
locked in a glass cabinet
some nights We stay up
passing it back and
forth
between us
drinking deep

Key Episodes from an Earthly Life

As surely as there are crumbs on the lips
of the blind   I came for a reason

I remember when the fields were no taller
than a pencil   do you remember that

I told him   I've got socks older than her
but he would not listen

You will starve out girl   they told her
but she did not listen

As surely as there is rice in the cuffs
of the priest   sex is a factor   not a fact

Everything I do is leaning   toward
what we came for   is that perfectly clear

I like your shoes your uncut hair
I like your use of space too

I wanted to knock her lights out
the air cut in and did us some good

One thing about my television set it has
a knob on it enabling me to switch channels

Now it is your turn   to shake or
provoke   or heal me   I won't say it again

Do you like your beets well-cooked and chilled
even if they make your gums itch

Those dark arkansas roads   that is the sound
I am after   the choiring of crickets

Around this time of year   especially evening
I love everything   I sold enough eggs

To buy a new dress   I watched him drink the juice
of our beets   And render the light liquid

I came to talk you into physical splendor
I do not wish to speak to your machine

Girl Friend Poem #3

She was white and flown
as a kleenex turning into a swan.
I lifted her veil; the face disappeared.
As if I had exposed some film
to sun. Twirling our skirts.
Laughing until the clouds sopped up
the light. And the peaches fell down around us.

for sharon

In a Piercing and Sucking Species

he doesn't see anybody
in the tree
nor does she see anybody

in the grass he wires
that wiring her
he gets erect

reading this very wire
in the grass
she gets wet

the presence of his absence
disturbs the absence
of his presence sometimes

more sometimes less
in dreams they go forward
without hunger without faces

others fall off the limb
but she does not fall
she pierces him

everywhere and nobody else

41

when she returns
she seizes him

in quivering mandibles
relieved
to find him

unchewed
newly in leaf

Crescent

In recent months I have become intent on seizing happiness: to this end I applied various shades of blue: only the evening is outside us now propagating honeysuckle: I am trying to invent a new way of moving under my dress: the room squares off against this: watch the water glitter with excitement: when we cut below the silver skin of the surface the center retains its fluidity: do I still remind you of a locust clinging to a branch: I give you an idea of the damages: you would let edges be edges: believe me: when their eyes poured over your long body of poetry I also was there: when they lay their hands on your glass shade I also was there: when they put their whole trust in your grace I had to step outside to get away from my cravenness: we have done these things to one another without benefit of a mirror: unlike the honeysuckle goodness does not overtake us: yet the thigh keeps quiet under nylon: later beneath the blueness of trees the future falls out of place: something always happens: draw nearer my dear: never fear: the world spins nightly toward its brightness and we are on it

Everything Good between
Men and Women

has been written in mud and butter
and barbecue sauce. The walls and
the floors used to be gorgeous.
The socks off-white and a near match.
The quince with fireblight
but we get two pints of jelly
in the end. Long walks strengthen
the back. You with a fever blister
and myself with a sty. Eyes
have we and we are forever prey
to one another's teeth. The torrents
go over us. Thunder has not harmed
anyone we know. The river coursing
through us is dirty and deep. The left
hand protects the rhythm. Watch
your head. No fires should be
unattended. Especially when wind. Each
receives a free swiss army knife.
The first few tongues are clearly
preparatory. The impression

made by yours I carry to my grave. It is
just so sad so creepy so beautiful.
Bless it. We have so little time
to learn, so much. . . . The river
courses dirty and deep. Cover the lettuce.
Call it a night. O soul. Flow on. Instead.

Girl Friend Poem #4

Together they marry the man
who will not wear gloves

In the morning they throw hair
from their brush out the window

Now the birds have enough for a nest

A lot is moving
in the frangible life of the soil

Amid the susurrus of grasses
one chair waits near another

The public is in ecstasy

for kate

The Iris Admits the Light
the Iris Will Allow

a letter flew into his hand
just like a bird into glass
undatable expressions
began crossing her face
he went up the ladder
to a heaven of solitude
an uneven seam of sunshine
stitched up her eyes

Like Someone Driving to Texas
by Herself

a car   that could not pass inspection   an expired license
like someone suddenly overtaken   with a need to see them
again   moving fast and in formation   she could feel
the white lines
streaming by   the radio tuned to the road   like someone
crying in the bathroom   she attacked her own idiom
welcomed
the distraction of corporeal detail   a toenail on the tile
some hair   the drain could not swallow   according to
the legend   not a long way to go   books thrashing
in the trunk   unpowered steering   the arduous turning
around
and skies   amassing at the border

words appeared
by which she wanted to live   not singularly but
companionate
in a wandering and guilty life   everyone makes
orthographic errors
while her face slept in her hand   her mind saw him
sitting at his oak plane   with his new pen

he wrote steadily into the night   thinking the next paragraph
            would surely snuff out   the destroying angel
thinking the sequel to the rain would be a gaining movement
            focused between two cones of light
                like someone driving to texas

Morning Star

This isn't the end. It simply
cannot be the end. It is a road.
You go ahead coatless, light-
soaked, more rutilant than
the road. The soles of your shoes
sparkle. You walk softly
as you move further inside
your subject. It is a living
season. The trees are anxious
to be included. The car with fins
beams through countless
oncoming points of rage and need.
The sloughed off cells
under our bed form little hills
of dead matter. If the most sidereal
drink is pain, the most soothing
clock is music. A poetry
of shine could come of this.
It will be predominantly
green. You will be allowed

to color in as much as you want
for green is good
for the teeth and the eyes.

Like Rocks

they surfaced   gradually   until the center cooled
male and female colored differently   like dinosaurs
colored by impurities   autochthonous
sprung from inner earth   or ancient seas
without names   sunscreen   honorary degrees
given the climate
and the silence   except for continuous wave action
intermittent screeches
a strange yelping   impervious to   oarlock
axstroke   gunstock   out of pressure   heat from above
and under

continuous wave action   impressed with ferns
quarry me   uplift   butterfly me   micturate
across the flat of my back
it had to be a dawn horse
crag   fracture   cleave
fingered   sniffed   specified
by luster   hardness   coarseness
the caught and faceted light

rubbed smooth   by continuous wave action
in the very beginning   was only fucking
    hunger   poetry   breath   shhhhhh

Privacy

The animals are leaving
the safety of the trees

Light sensors respond
to the footfall of every guest

To retard the growth of algae

The fishes must be moved
from the window

Stiller than water she lay
As in a glass dress

As if all life might come to its end
within the radius of her bed

Beyond the reef of trees a beach cannot be seen
The bay itself barely breathing

In the other wing of the house
A small boat awaits elucidation

Girl Friend Poem #5

The brunette is boarding a train
with many bundles

The pockets are sewn shut on
her rayon jacket

The old world tapers away

The day slips through the straw
whole as an egg

We use Gregg shorthand
so the men won't understand

The brunette has traveled over 700 versts

A breath parts her lips

Let's nurse one another's babies
She says even before

We tell what we've been reading

for shelby

Ponds, in Love

One was always going when the other was coming back
One was biting a green apple
The deeper the evening the louder the singing
Throwing the core out the window
An oar stirred the dark and then quit
A face drenches itself in carlight
A wrist wearing a man's watch dipped a net
Even as one turned toward an unfinished building
The other wondered what one would have on
Upon returning will the hair be fallen or cropped
If one reaches what is grasped for
Gnats go for the eyes
Will utter disappointment set in
Will it be water or milk or wine tonight
Mostly one listened in the low intensity glow
Of events one sustains incomprehensible feelings

Like Horses

in their long black coat   they love the back roads
show their teeth   in a heartbeat   breathe in breathe out
don't fool around with them   their involuntary nervousness
beasts   of draft and burden   they are naturally
nervous   saps for the sweet sop   left buttock rubbed
against bark   and barbed wire
she ungulates   whence their fire   sweat like ballerinas
and stink   during the intervals
cannot help but be anxious   for the morrow   don't trust
anybody
they are helpless lying down

the young husband stands
on one foot   in front of the blackboard   the wet banged
equestrian students   breathe in breathe out   the sugar apple
on his desk   cannot help but be anxious
for the morrow
he ungulates   don't trust anybody   never have
they never will

57

Flame

the breath	the trees	the bridge
the road	the rain	the sheen
the breath	the line	the skin
the vineyard	the fences	the leg
the water	the breath	the shift
the hair	the wheels	the shoulder
the breath	the lane	the streak
the lining	the hour	the reasons
the name	the distance	the breath
the scent	the dogs	the blear
the lungs	the breath	the glove
the signal	the turn	the need
the steps	the lights	the door
the mouth	the tongue	the eyes
the burn	the burned	the burning

Girl Friend Poem #6

When I snap my fingers
You will wake in a dear yet unfamiliar place
You will scarcely remember your travail
You will be eating green caterpillars over a small fire
An awesome congeries of youthful men and women
   Will be brushing these very tracks away

for debbie

ABOUT THE AUTHOR

C.D. Wright was born and raised in the Ozark Mountains of Arkansas. She has published seven collections of poetry, most recently *Just Whistle*, a book length poem in collaboration with the photographer Deborah Luster. In 1994 she was named State Poet of Rhode Island, a five-year post. On a fellowship for writers from the Lila Wallace-Reader's Digest Foundation, she curated "a walk-in book of Arkansas" an exhibition now touring throughout her native state. Wright is on the faculty at Brown University. She is the co-editor of Lost Roads Publishers with the poet Forrest Gander. They live with their son Brecht near Providence, Rhode Island.